Release it

An Author's Book for Release Date Information

Book Title: ___________________________

Release Date: ___________________________

Cover Reveal: ___________________________

ARC Release: ___________________________

Send to Pre-Reader(s) By: ___________________________

Send to Blogs By: ___________________________

Send to Betas By: ___________________________

Send to Editor By: ___________________________

Send to Formatter By: ___________________________

Set Up Pre-Order/Release By: ___________________________

Final Cover Design Needed By: ___________________________

Upload By: ___________________________

Extra Notes:

____

____

____

____

Book Title: _______________________________

Release Date: _______________________________

Cover Reveal: _______________________________

ARC Release: _______________________________

Send to Pre-Reader(s) By: _______________________________

Send to Blogs By: _______________________________

Send to Betas By: _______________________________

Send to Editor By: _______________________________

Send to Formatter By: _______________________________

Set Up Pre-Order/Release By: _______________________________

Final Cover Design Needed By: _______________________________

Upload By: _______________________________

Extra Notes:

____

____

____

____

Book Title: _______________________________

Release Date: _______________________________

Cover Reveal: _______________________________

ARC Release: _______________________________

Send to Pre-Reader(s) By: _______________________________

Send to Blogs By: _______________________________

Send to Betas By: _______________________________

Send to Editor By: _______________________________

Send to Formatter By: _______________________________

Set Up Pre-Order/Release By: _______________________________

Final Cover Design Needed By: _______________________________

Upload By: _______________________________

Extra Notes:

____

____

____

____

____

Book Title: _______________________________

Release Date: _______________________________

Cover Reveal: _______________________________

ARC Release: _______________________________

Send to Pre-Reader(s) By: _______________________________

Send to Blogs By: _______________________________

Send to Betas By: _______________________________

Send to Editor By: _______________________________

Send to Formatter By: _______________________________

Set Up Pre-Order/Release By: _______________________________

Final Cover Design Needed By: _______________________________

Upload By: _______________________________

Extra Notes:

____

____

____

____

____

Book Title: _______________________________________

Release Date: _______________________________________

Cover Reveal: _______________________________________

ARC Release: _______________________________________

Send to Pre-Reader(s) By: _______________________________________

Send to Blogs By: _______________________________________

Send to Betas By: _______________________________________

Send to Editor By: _______________________________________

Send to Formatter By: _______________________________________

Set Up Pre-Order/Release By: _______________________________________

Final Cover Design Needed By: _______________________________________

Upload By: _______________________________________

Extra Notes:

____

____

____

____

Book Title: ___________________________

Release Date: ___________________________

Cover Reveal: ___________________________

ARC Release: ___________________________

Send to Pre-Reader(s) By: ___________________________

Send to Blogs By: ___________________________

Send to Betas By: ___________________________

Send to Editor By: ___________________________

Send to Formatter By: ___________________________

Set Up Pre-Order/Release By: ___________________________

Final Cover Design Needed By: ___________________________

Upload By: ___________________________

Extra Notes:

____

____

____

____

Book Title: ____________________________________

Release Date: ____________________________________

Cover Reveal: ____________________________________

ARC Release: ____________________________________

Send to Pre-Reader(s) By: ____________________________________

Send to Blogs By: ____________________________________

Send to Betas By: ____________________________________

Send to Editor By: ____________________________________

Send to Formatter By: ____________________________________

Set Up Pre-Order/Release By: ____________________________________

Final Cover Design Needed By: ____________________________________

Upload By: ____________________________________

Extra Notes:

____

____

____

____

____

Book Title: ______________________________

Release Date: ______________________________

Cover Reveal: ______________________________

ARC Release: ______________________________

Send to Pre-Reader(s) By: ______________________________

Send to Blogs By: ______________________________

Send to Betas By: ______________________________

Send to Editor By: ______________________________

Send to Formatter By: ______________________________

Set Up Pre-Order/Release By: ______________________________

Final Cover Design Needed By: ______________________________

Upload By: ______________________________

Extra Notes:

____

____

____

____

BOOK TITLE: _______________________________

RELEASE DATE: _______________________________

COVER REVEAL: _______________________________

ARC RELEASE: _______________________________

SEND TO PRE-READER(S) BY: _______________________________

SEND TO BLOGS BY: _______________________________

SEND TO BETAS BY: _______________________________

SEND TO EDITOR BY: _______________________________

SEND TO FORMATTER BY: _______________________________

SET UP PRE-ORDER/RELEASE BY: _______________________________

FINAL COVER DESIGN NEEDED BY: _______________________________

UPLOAD BY: _______________________________

EXTRA NOTES:

____

____

____

____

Book Title: _______________________________

Release Date: _______________________________

Cover Reveal: _______________________________

ARC Release: _______________________________

Send to Pre-Reader(s) By: _______________________________

Send to Blogs By: _______________________________

Send to Betas By: _______________________________

Send to Editor By: _______________________________

Send to Formatter By: _______________________________

Set Up Pre-Order/Release By: _______________________________

Final Cover Design Needed By: _______________________________

Upload By: _______________________________

Extra Notes:

____

____

____

____

Book Title: ___________________________________

Release Date: ___________________________________

Cover Reveal: ___________________________________

ARC Release: ___________________________________

Send to Pre-Reader(s) By: ___________________________________

Send to Blogs By: ___________________________________

Send to Betas By: ___________________________________

Send to Editor By: ___________________________________

Send to Formatter By: ___________________________________

Set Up Pre-Order/Release By: ___________________________________

Final Cover Design Needed By: ___________________________________

Upload By: ___________________________________

Extra Notes:

____

____

____

____

____

Book Title: ___________________________

Release Date: ___________________________

Cover Reveal: ___________________________

ARC Release: ___________________________

Send to Pre-Reader(s) By: ___________________________

Send to Blogs By: ___________________________

Send to Betas By: ___________________________

Send to Editor By: ___________________________

Send to Formatter By: ___________________________

Set Up Pre-Order/Release By: ___________________________

Final Cover Design Needed By: ___________________________

Upload By: ___________________________

Extra Notes:

____

____

____

____

____

Book Title: _______________________________

Release Date: _______________________________

Cover Reveal: _______________________________

ARC Release: _______________________________

Send to Pre-Reader(s) By: _______________________________

Send to Blogs By: _______________________________

Send to Betas By: _______________________________

Send to Editor By: _______________________________

Send to Formatter By: _______________________________

Set Up Pre-Order/Release By: _______________________________

Final Cover Design Needed By: _______________________________

Upload By: _______________________________

Extra Notes:

____

____

____

____

Book Title: _______________________________

Release Date: _______________________________

Cover Reveal: _______________________________

ARC Release: _______________________________

Send to Pre-Reader(s) By: _______________________________

Send to Blogs By: _______________________________

Send to Betas By: _______________________________

Send to Editor By: _______________________________

Send to Formatter By: _______________________________

Set Up Pre-Order/Release By: _______________________________

Final Cover Design Needed By: _______________________________

Upload By: _______________________________

Extra Notes:

____

____

____

____

____

Book Title: _______________________________

Release Date: _______________________________

Cover Reveal: _______________________________

ARC Release: _______________________________

Send to Pre-Reader(s) By: _______________________________

Send to Blogs By: _______________________________

Send to Betas By: _______________________________

Send to Editor By: _______________________________

Send to Formatter By: _______________________________

Set Up Pre-Order/Release By: _______________________________

Final Cover Design Needed By: _______________________________

Upload By: _______________________________

Extra Notes:

____

____

____

____

____

Book Title: ________________________

Release Date: ________________________

Cover Reveal: ________________________

ARC Release: ________________________

Send to Pre-Reader(s) By: ________________________

Send to Blogs By: ________________________

Send to Betas By: ________________________

Send to Editor By: ________________________

Send to Formatter By: ________________________

Set Up Pre-Order/Release By: ________________________

Final Cover Design Needed By: ________________________

Upload By: ________________________

Extra Notes:

____

____

____

____

Book Title: _______________________________

Release Date: _______________________________

Cover Reveal: _______________________________

ARC Release: _______________________________

Send to Pre-Reader(s) By: _______________________________

Send to Blogs By: _______________________________

Send to Betas By: _______________________________

Send to Editor By: _______________________________

Send to Formatter By: _______________________________

Set Up Pre-Order/Release By: _______________________________

Final Cover Design Needed By: _______________________________

Upload By: _______________________________

Extra Notes:

____

____

____

____

____

Book Title: _______________________________

Release Date: _______________________________

Cover Reveal: _______________________________

ARC Release: _______________________________

Send to Pre-Reader(s) By: _______________________________

Send to Blogs By: _______________________________

Send to Betas By: _______________________________

Send to Editor By: _______________________________

Send to Formatter By: _______________________________

Set Up Pre-Order/Release By: _______________________________

Final Cover Design Needed By: _______________________________

Upload By: _______________________________

Extra Notes:

____

____

____

____

____

Book Title: _______________________________________

Release Date: _______________________________________

Cover Reveal: _______________________________________

ARC Release: _______________________________________

Send to Pre-Reader(s) By: _______________________________________

Send to Blogs By: _______________________________________

Send to Betas By: _______________________________________

Send to Editor By: _______________________________________

Send to Formatter By: _______________________________________

Set Up Pre-Order/Release By: _______________________________________

Final Cover Design Needed By: _______________________________________

Upload By: _______________________________________

Extra Notes:

____

____

____

____

Book Title: _______________________________

Release Date: _______________________________

Cover Reveal: _______________________________

ARC Release: _______________________________

Send to Pre-Reader(s) By: _______________________________

Send to Blogs By: _______________________________

Send to Betas By: _______________________________

Send to Editor By: _______________________________

Send to Formatter By: _______________________________

Set Up Pre-Order/Release By: _______________________________

Final Cover Design Needed By: _______________________________

Upload By: _______________________________

Extra Notes:

____

____

____

____

____

Book Title: ____

Release Date: ____

Cover Reveal: ____

ARC Release: ____

Send to Pre-Reader(s) By: ____

Send to Blogs By: ____

Send to Betas By: ____

Send to Editor By: ____

Send to Formatter By: ____

Set Up Pre-Order/Release By: ____

Final Cover Design Needed By: ____

Upload By: ____

Extra Notes:

____

____

____

____

____

Book Title: _______________________________

Release Date: _______________________________

Cover Reveal: _______________________________

ARC Release: _______________________________

Send to Pre-Reader(s) By: _______________________________

Send to Blogs By: _______________________________

Send to Betas By: _______________________________

Send to Editor By: _______________________________

Send to Formatter By: _______________________________

Set Up Pre-Order/Release By: _______________________________

Final Cover Design Needed By: _______________________________

Upload By: _______________________________

Extra Notes:

____

____

____

____

____

Book Title: _______________________________

Release Date: _______________________________

Cover Reveal: _______________________________

ARC Release: _______________________________

Send to Pre-Reader(s) By: _______________________________

Send to Blogs By: _______________________________

Send to Betas By: _______________________________

Send to Editor By: _______________________________

Send to Formatter By: _______________________________

Set Up Pre-Order/Release By: _______________________________

Final Cover Design Needed By: _______________________________

Upload By: _______________________________

Extra Notes:

____

____

____

____

Book Title: _______________________________

Release Date: _______________________________

Cover Reveal: _______________________________

ARC Release: _______________________________

Send to Pre-Reader(s) By: _______________________________

Send to Blogs By: _______________________________

Send to Betas By: _______________________________

Send to Editor By: _______________________________

Send to Formatter By: _______________________________

Set Up Pre-Order/Release By: _______________________________

Final Cover Design Needed By: _______________________________

Upload By: _______________________________

Extra Notes:

____

____

____

____

____

Book Title: _______________________________

Release Date: _______________________________

Cover Reveal: _______________________________

ARC Release: _______________________________

Send to Pre-Reader(s) By: _______________________________

Send to Blogs By: _______________________________

Send to Betas By: _______________________________

Send to Editor By: _______________________________

Send to Formatter By: _______________________________

Set Up Pre-Order/Release By: _______________________________

Final Cover Design Needed By: _______________________________

Upload By: _______________________________

Extra Notes:

____

____

____

____

Book Title: _______________________________

Release Date: _______________________________

Cover Reveal: _______________________________

ARC Release: _______________________________

Send to Pre-Reader(s) By: _______________________________

Send to Blogs By: _______________________________

Send to Betas By: _______________________________

Send to Editor By: _______________________________

Send to Formatter By: _______________________________

Set Up Pre-Order/Release By: _______________________________

Final Cover Design Needed By: _______________________________

Upload By: _______________________________

Extra Notes:

____

____

____

____

____

Book Title: _______________________________

Release Date: _______________________________

Cover Reveal: _______________________________

ARC Release: _______________________________

Send to Pre-Reader(s) By: _______________________________

Send to Blogs By: _______________________________

Send to Betas By: _______________________________

Send to Editor By: _______________________________

Send to Formatter By: _______________________________

Set Up Pre-Order/Release By: _______________________________

Final Cover Design Needed By: _______________________________

Upload By: _______________________________

Extra Notes:

____

____

____

____

____

Book Title: _______________________________

Release Date: _______________________________

Cover Reveal: _______________________________

ARC Release: _______________________________

Send to Pre-Reader(s) By: _______________________________

Send to Blogs By: _______________________________

Send to Betas By: _______________________________

Send to Editor By: _______________________________

Send to Formatter By: _______________________________

Set Up Pre-Order/Release By: _______________________________

Final Cover Design Needed By: _______________________________

Upload By: _______________________________

Extra Notes:

____

____

____

____

____

Book Title: _______________________________

Release Date: _______________________________

Cover Reveal: _______________________________

ARC Release: _______________________________

Send to Pre-Reader(s) By: _______________________________

Send to Blogs By: _______________________________

Send to Betas By: _______________________________

Send to Editor By: _______________________________

Send to Formatter By: _______________________________

Set Up Pre-Order/Release By: _______________________________

Final Cover Design Needed By: _______________________________

Upload By: _______________________________

Extra Notes:

____

____

____

____

Book Title: _______________________________

Release Date: _______________________________

Cover Reveal: _______________________________

ARC Release: _______________________________

Send to Pre-Reader(s) By: _______________________________

Send to Blogs By: _______________________________

Send to Betas By: _______________________________

Send to Editor By: _______________________________

Send to Formatter By: _______________________________

Set Up Pre-Order/Release By: _______________________________

Final Cover Design Needed By: _______________________________

Upload By: _______________________________

Extra Notes:

____

____

____

____

Book Title: ________________________________

Release Date: ________________________________

Cover Reveal: ________________________________

ARC Release: ________________________________

Send to Pre-Reader(s) By: ________________________________

Send to Blogs By: ________________________________

Send to Betas By: ________________________________

Send to Editor By: ________________________________

Send to Formatter By: ________________________________

Set Up Pre-Order/Release By: ________________________________

Final Cover Design Needed By: ________________________________

Upload By: ________________________________

Extra Notes:

____

____

____

____

____

Book Title: ______________________________

Release Date: ______________________________

Cover Reveal: ______________________________

ARC Release: ______________________________

Send to Pre-Reader(s) By: ______________________________

Send to Blogs By: ______________________________

Send to Betas By: ______________________________

Send to Editor By: ______________________________

Send to Formatter By: ______________________________

Set Up Pre-Order/Release By: ______________________________

Final Cover Design Needed By: ______________________________

Upload By: ______________________________

Extra Notes:

____

____

____

____

Book Title: _________________________________

Release Date: _________________________________

Cover Reveal: _________________________________

ARC Release: _________________________________

Send to Pre-Reader(s) By: _________________________________

Send to Blogs By: _________________________________

Send to Betas By: _________________________________

Send to Editor By: _________________________________

Send to Formatter By: _________________________________

Set Up Pre-Order/Release By: _________________________________

Final Cover Design Needed By: _________________________________

Upload By: _________________________________

Extra Notes:

____

____

____

____

Book Title: ______________________________

Release Date: ______________________________

Cover Reveal: ______________________________

ARC Release: ______________________________

Send to Pre-Reader(s) By: ______________________________

Send to Blogs By: ______________________________

Send to Betas By: ______________________________

Send to Editor By: ______________________________

Send to Formatter By: ______________________________

Set Up Pre-Order/Release By: ______________________________

Final Cover Design Needed By: ______________________________

Upload By: ______________________________

Extra Notes:

____

____

____

____

Book Title: _______________________________

Release Date: _______________________________

Cover Reveal: _______________________________

ARC Release: _______________________________

Send to Pre-Reader(s) By: _______________________________

Send to Blogs By: _______________________________

Send to Betas By: _______________________________

Send to Editor By: _______________________________

Send to Formatter By: _______________________________

Set Up Pre-Order/Release By: _______________________________

Final Cover Design Needed By: _______________________________

Upload By: _______________________________

Extra Notes:

____

____

____

____

____

Book Title: ______________________________

Release Date: ______________________________

Cover Reveal: ______________________________

ARC Release: ______________________________

Send to Pre-Reader(s) By: ______________________________

Send to Blogs By: ______________________________

Send to Betas By: ______________________________

Send to Editor By: ______________________________

Send to Formatter By: ______________________________

Set Up Pre-Order/Release By: ______________________________

Final Cover Design Needed By: ______________________________

Upload By: ______________________________

Extra Notes:

____

____

____

____

____

Book Title: ______________________________

Release Date: ______________________________

Cover Reveal: ______________________________

ARC Release: ______________________________

Send to Pre-Reader(s) By: ______________________________

Send to Blogs By: ______________________________

Send to Betas By: ______________________________

Send to Editor By: ______________________________

Send to Formatter By: ______________________________

Set Up Pre-Order/Release By: ______________________________

Final Cover Design Needed By: ______________________________

Upload By: ______________________________

Extra Notes:

____

____

____

____

Book Title: _________________________

Release Date: _________________________

Cover Reveal: _________________________

ARC Release: _________________________

Send to Pre-Reader(s) By: _________________________

Send to Blogs By: _________________________

Send to Betas By: _________________________

Send to Editor By: _________________________

Send to Formatter By: _________________________

Set Up Pre-Order/Release By: _________________________

Final Cover Design Needed By: _________________________

Upload By: _________________________

Extra Notes:

____

____

____

____

Book Title: _______________________

Release Date: _______________________

Cover Reveal: _______________________

ARC Release: _______________________

Send to Pre-Reader(s) By: _______________________

Send to Blogs By: _______________________

Send to Betas By: _______________________

Send to Editor By: _______________________

Send to Formatter By: _______________________

Set Up Pre-Order/Release By: _______________________

Final Cover Design Needed By: _______________________

Upload By: _______________________

Extra Notes:

____

____

____

____

Book Title: _______________________

Release Date: _______________________

Cover Reveal: _______________________

ARC Release: _______________________

Send to Pre-Reader(s) By: _______________________

Send to Blogs By: _______________________

Send to Betas By: _______________________

Send to Editor By: _______________________

Send to Formatter By: _______________________

Set Up Pre-Order/Release By: _______________________

Final Cover Design Needed By: _______________________

Upload By: _______________________

Extra Notes:

____

____

____

____

____

Book Title: _______________________________

Release Date: _______________________________

Cover Reveal: _______________________________

ARC Release: _______________________________

Send to Pre-Reader(s) By: _______________________________

Send to Blogs By: _______________________________

Send to Betas By: _______________________________

Send to Editor By: _______________________________

Send to Formatter By: _______________________________

Set Up Pre-Order/Release By: _______________________________

Final Cover Design Needed By: _______________________________

Upload By: _______________________________

Extra Notes:

____

____

____

____

____

Book Title: ______________________________

Release Date: ______________________________

Cover Reveal: ______________________________

ARC Release: ______________________________

Send to Pre-Reader(s) By: ______________________________

Send to Blogs By: ______________________________

Send to Betas By: ______________________________

Send to Editor By: ______________________________

Send to Formatter By: ______________________________

Set Up Pre-Order/Release By: ______________________________

Final Cover Design Needed By: ______________________________

Upload By: ______________________________

Extra Notes:

____

____

____

____

____

Book Title: _______________________________

Release Date: _______________________________

Cover Reveal: _______________________________

ARC Release: _______________________________

Send to Pre-Reader(s) By: _______________________________

Send to Blogs By: _______________________________

Send to Betas By: _______________________________

Send to Editor By: _______________________________

Send to Formatter By: _______________________________

Set Up Pre-Order/Release By: _______________________________

Final Cover Design Needed By: _______________________________

Upload By: _______________________________

Extra Notes:

____

____

____

____

____

Book Title:
____

Release Date:
____

Cover Reveal:
____

ARC Release:
____

Send to Pre-Reader(s) By:
____

Send to Blogs By:
____

Send to Betas By:
____

Send to Editor By:
____

Send to Formatter By:
____

Set Up Pre-Order/Release By:
____

Final Cover Design Needed By:
____

Upload By:
____

Extra Notes:
____

____

____

____

Book Title: _______________________________

Release Date: _______________________________

Cover Reveal: _______________________________

ARC Release: _______________________________

Send to Pre-Reader(s) By: _______________________________

Send to Blogs By: _______________________________

Send to Betas By: _______________________________

Send to Editor By: _______________________________

Send to Formatter By: _______________________________

Set Up Pre-Order/Release By: _______________________________

Final Cover Design Needed By: _______________________________

Upload By: _______________________________

Extra Notes:

____

____

____

____

____

Book Title: ___________________________

Release Date: ___________________________

Cover Reveal: ___________________________

ARC Release: ___________________________

Send to Pre-Reader(s) By: ___________________________

Send to Blogs By: ___________________________

Send to Betas By: ___________________________

Send to Editor By: ___________________________

Send to Formatter By: ___________________________

Set Up Pre-Order/Release By: ___________________________

Final Cover Design Needed By: ___________________________

Upload By: ___________________________

Extra Notes:

____

____

____

____

Book Title: ______________________________

Release Date: ______________________________

Cover Reveal: ______________________________

ARC Release: ______________________________

Send to Pre-Reader(s) By: ______________________________

Send to Blogs By: ______________________________

Send to Betas By: ______________________________

Send to Editor By: ______________________________

Send to Formatter By: ______________________________

Set Up Pre-Order/Release By: ______________________________

Final Cover Design Needed By: ______________________________

Upload By: ______________________________

Extra Notes:

____

____

____

____

____

Book Title: _______________________

Release Date: _______________________

Cover Reveal: _______________________

ARC Release: _______________________

Send to Pre-Reader(s) By: _______________________

Send to Blogs By: _______________________

Send to Betas By: _______________________

Send to Editor By: _______________________

Send to Formatter By: _______________________

Set Up Pre-Order/Release By: _______________________

Final Cover Design Needed By: _______________________

Upload By: _______________________

Extra Notes:

____

____

____

____

____

BOOK TITLE: ___________________________________

RELEASE DATE: ___________________________________

COVER REVEAL: ___________________________________

ARC RELEASE: ___________________________________

SEND TO PRE-READER(S) BY: ___________________________________

SEND TO BLOGS BY: ___________________________________

SEND TO BETAS BY: ___________________________________

SEND TO EDITOR BY: ___________________________________

SEND TO FORMATTER BY: ___________________________________

SET UP PRE-ORDER/RELEASE BY: ___________________________________

FINAL COVER DESIGN NEEDED BY: ___________________________________

UPLOAD BY: ___________________________________

EXTRA NOTES:

____

____

____

____

Book Title: _______________________________

Release Date: _______________________________

Cover Reveal: _______________________________

ARC Release: _______________________________

Send to Pre-Reader(s) By: _______________________________

Send to Blogs By: _______________________________

Send to Betas By: _______________________________

Send to Editor By: _______________________________

Send to Formatter By: _______________________________

Set Up Pre-Order/Release By: _______________________________

Final Cover Design Needed By: _______________________________

Upload By: _______________________________

Extra Notes:

____

____

____

____

____

Book Title: ______________________________

Release Date: ______________________________

Cover Reveal: ______________________________

ARC Release: ______________________________

Send to Pre-Reader(s) By: ______________________________

Send to Blogs By: ______________________________

Send to Betas By: ______________________________

Send to Editor By: ______________________________

Send to Formatter By: ______________________________

Set Up Pre-Order/Release By: ______________________________

Final Cover Design Needed By: ______________________________

Upload By: ______________________________

Extra Notes:

____

____

____

____

____

Book Title: _______________________________

Release Date: _______________________________

Cover Reveal: _______________________________

ARC Release: _______________________________

Send to Pre-Reader(s) By: _______________________________

Send to Blogs By: _______________________________

Send to Betas By: _______________________________

Send to Editor By: _______________________________

Send to Formatter By: _______________________________

Set Up Pre-Order/Release By: _______________________________

Final Cover Design Needed By: _______________________________

Upload By: _______________________________

Extra Notes:

____

____

____

____

____

Book Title: _______________________________

Release Date: _______________________________

Cover Reveal: _______________________________

ARC Release: _______________________________

Send to Pre-Reader(s) By: _______________________________

Send to Blogs By: _______________________________

Send to Betas By: _______________________________

Send to Editor By: _______________________________

Send to Formatter By: _______________________________

Set Up Pre-Order/Release By: _______________________________

Final Cover Design Needed By: _______________________________

Upload By: _______________________________

Extra Notes:

____

____

____

____

Book Title: ________________________

Release Date: ________________________

Cover Reveal: ________________________

ARC Release: ________________________

Send to Pre-Reader(s) By: ________________________

Send to Blogs By: ________________________

Send to Betas By: ________________________

Send to Editor By: ________________________

Send to Formatter By: ________________________

Set Up Pre-Order/Release By: ________________________

Final Cover Design Needed By: ________________________

Upload By: ________________________

Extra Notes:

____

____

____

____

____

Book Title: _______________________________________

Release Date: _______________________________________

Cover Reveal: _______________________________________

ARC Release: _______________________________________

Send to Pre-Reader(s) By: _______________________________________

Send to Blogs By: _______________________________________

Send to Betas By: _______________________________________

Send to Editor By: _______________________________________

Send to Formatter By: _______________________________________

Set Up Pre-Order/Release By: _______________________________________

Final Cover Design Needed By: _______________________________________

Upload By: _______________________________________

Extra Notes:

____

____

____

____

____

BOOK TITLE: ____________________________

RELEASE DATE: ____________________________

COVER REVEAL: ____________________________

ARC RELEASE: ____________________________

SEND TO PRE-READER(S) BY: ____________________________

SEND TO BLOGS BY: ____________________________

SEND TO BETAS BY: ____________________________

SEND TO EDITOR BY: ____________________________

SEND TO FORMATTER BY: ____________________________

SET UP PRE-ORDER/RELEASE BY: ____________________________

FINAL COVER DESIGN NEEDED BY: ____________________________

UPLOAD BY: ____________________________

EXTRA NOTES:

____

____

____

____

____

Book Title: ______________________________

Release Date: ______________________________

Cover Reveal: ______________________________

ARC Release: ______________________________

Send to Pre-Reader(s) By: ______________________________

Send to Blogs By: ______________________________

Send to Betas By: ______________________________

Send to Editor By: ______________________________

Send to Formatter By: ______________________________

Set Up Pre-Order/Release By: ______________________________

Final Cover Design Needed By: ______________________________

Upload By: ______________________________

Extra Notes:

____

____

____

____

____

Book Title: _______________________________

Release Date: _______________________________

Cover Reveal: _______________________________

ARC Release: _______________________________

Send to Pre-Reader(s) By: _______________________________

Send to Blogs By: _______________________________

Send to Betas By: _______________________________

Send to Editor By: _______________________________

Send to Formatter By: _______________________________

Set Up Pre-Order/Release By: _______________________________

Final Cover Design Needed By: _______________________________

Upload By: _______________________________

Extra Notes:

____

____

____

____

____

Book Title: _______________________________

Release Date: _______________________________

Cover Reveal: _______________________________

ARC Release: _______________________________

Send to Pre-Reader(s) By: _______________________________

Send to Blogs By: _______________________________

Send to Betas By: _______________________________

Send to Editor By: _______________________________

Send to Formatter By: _______________________________

Set Up Pre-Order/Release By: _______________________________

Final Cover Design Needed By: _______________________________

Upload By: _______________________________

Extra Notes:

____

____

____

____

Book Title: ______________________________

Release Date: ______________________________

Cover Reveal: ______________________________

ARC Release: ______________________________

Send to Pre-Reader(s) By: ______________________________

Send to Blogs By: ______________________________

Send to Betas By: ______________________________

Send to Editor By: ______________________________

Send to Formatter By: ______________________________

Set Up Pre-Order/Release By: ______________________________

Final Cover Design Needed By: ______________________________

Upload By: ______________________________

Extra Notes:

____

____

____

____

____

Book Title: ______________________________

Release Date: ______________________________

Cover Reveal: ______________________________

ARC Release: ______________________________

Send to Pre-Reader(s) By: ______________________________

Send to Blogs By: ______________________________

Send to Betas By: ______________________________

Send to Editor By: ______________________________

Send to Formatter By: ______________________________

Set Up Pre-Order/Release By: ______________________________

Final Cover Design Needed By: ______________________________

Upload By: ______________________________

Extra Notes:

____

____

____

____

____

Book Title: ______________________________

Release Date: ______________________________

Cover Reveal: ______________________________

ARC Release: ______________________________

Send to Pre-Reader(s) By: ______________________________

Send to Blogs By: ______________________________

Send to Betas By: ______________________________

Send to Editor By: ______________________________

Send to Formatter By: ______________________________

Set Up Pre-Order/Release By: ______________________________

Final Cover Design Needed By: ______________________________

Upload By: ______________________________

Extra Notes:

____

____

____

____

____

Book Title: _______________________________

Release Date: _______________________________

Cover Reveal: _______________________________

ARC Release: _______________________________

Send to Pre-Reader(s) By: _______________________________

Send to Blogs By: _______________________________

Send to Betas By: _______________________________

Send to Editor By: _______________________________

Send to Formatter By: _______________________________

Set Up Pre-Order/Release By: _______________________________

Final Cover Design Needed By: _______________________________

Upload By: _______________________________

Extra Notes:

____

____

____

____

Book Title: _______________________________

Release Date: _______________________________

Cover Reveal: _______________________________

ARC Release: _______________________________

Send to Pre-Reader(s) By: _______________________________

Send to Blogs By: _______________________________

Send to Betas By: _______________________________

Send to Editor By: _______________________________

Send to Formatter By: _______________________________

Set Up Pre-Order/Release By: _______________________________

Final Cover Design Needed By: _______________________________

Upload By: _______________________________

Extra Notes:

____

____

____

____

Book Title: ___________________________

Release Date: ___________________________

Cover Reveal: ___________________________

ARC Release: ___________________________

Send to Pre-Reader(s) By: ___________________________

Send to Blogs By: ___________________________

Send to Betas By: ___________________________

Send to Editor By: ___________________________

Send to Formatter By: ___________________________

Set Up Pre-Order/Release By: ___________________________

Final Cover Design Needed By: ___________________________

Upload By: ___________________________

Extra Notes:

____

____

____

____

Book Title: ______________________________________

Release Date: ___________________________________

Cover Reveal: ___________________________________

ARC Release: ____________________________________

Send to Pre-Reader(s) By: _________________________

Send to Blogs By: _______________________________

Send to Betas By: _______________________________

Send to Editor By: ______________________________

Send to Formatter By: ___________________________

Set Up Pre-Order/Release By: ______________________

Final Cover Design Needed By: _____________________

Upload By: ____________________________________

Extra Notes:

____

____

____

____

BOOK TITLE: ______________________________

RELEASE DATE: ______________________________

COVER REVEAL: ______________________________

ARC RELEASE: ______________________________

SEND TO PRE-READER(S) BY: ______________________________

SEND TO BLOGS BY: ______________________________

SEND TO BETAS BY: ______________________________

SEND TO EDITOR BY: ______________________________

SEND TO FORMATTER BY: ______________________________

SET UP PRE-ORDER/RELEASE BY: ______________________________

FINAL COVER DESIGN NEEDED BY: ______________________________

UPLOAD BY: ______________________________

EXTRA NOTES:

____

____

____

____

____

BOOK TITLE: ____

RELEASE DATE: ____

COVER REVEAL: ____

ARC RELEASE: ____

SEND TO PRE-READER(S) BY: _____________________________

SEND TO BLOGS BY: _____________________________________

SEND TO BETAS BY: _____________________________________

SEND TO EDITOR BY: ____________________________________

SEND TO FORMATTER BY: _________________________________

SET UP PRE-ORDER/RELEASE BY: __________________________

FINAL COVER DESIGN NEEDED BY: _________________________

UPLOAD BY: ____

EXTRA NOTES:

____

____

____

____

Book Title: _______________________________

Release Date: _______________________________

Cover Reveal: _______________________________

ARC Release: _______________________________

Send to Pre-Reader(s) By: _______________________________

Send to Blogs By: _______________________________

Send to Betas By: _______________________________

Send to Editor By: _______________________________

Send to Formatter By: _______________________________

Set Up Pre-Order/Release By: _______________________________

Final Cover Design Needed By: _______________________________

Upload By: _______________________________

Extra Notes:

____

____

____

____

Book Title: _______________________________

Release Date: _______________________________

Cover Reveal: _______________________________

ARC Release: _______________________________

Send to Pre-Reader(s) By: _______________________________

Send to Blogs By: _______________________________

Send to Betas By: _______________________________

Send to Editor By: _______________________________

Send to Formatter By: _______________________________

Set Up Pre-Order/Release By: _______________________________

Final Cover Design Needed By: _______________________________

Upload By: _______________________________

Extra Notes:

____

____

____

____

____

Book Title: ______________________________

Release Date: ______________________________

Cover Reveal: ______________________________

ARC Release: ______________________________

Send to Pre-Reader(s) By: ______________________________

Send to Blogs By: ______________________________

Send to Betas By: ______________________________

Send to Editor By: ______________________________

Send to Formatter By: ______________________________

Set Up Pre-Order/Release By: ______________________________

Final Cover Design Needed By: ______________________________

Upload By: ______________________________

Extra Notes:

____

____

____

____

Book Title: ______________________________

Release Date: ______________________________

Cover Reveal: ______________________________

ARC Release: ______________________________

Send to Pre-Reader(s) By: ______________________________

Send to Blogs By: ______________________________

Send to Betas By: ______________________________

Send to Editor By: ______________________________

Send to Formatter By: ______________________________

Set Up Pre-Order/Release By: ______________________________

Final Cover Design Needed By: ______________________________

Upload By: ______________________________

Extra Notes:

____

____

____

____

Book Title: ___________________________

Release Date: ___________________________

Cover Reveal: ___________________________

ARC Release: ___________________________

Send to Pre-Reader(s) By: ___________________________

Send to Blogs By: ___________________________

Send to Betas By: ___________________________

Send to Editor By: ___________________________

Send to Formatter By: ___________________________

Set Up Pre-Order/Release By: ___________________________

Final Cover Design Needed By: ___________________________

Upload By: ___________________________

Extra Notes:

____

____

____

____

____

Book Title: _______________________________

Release Date: _______________________________

Cover Reveal: _______________________________

ARC Release: _______________________________

Send to Pre-Reader(s) By: _______________________________

Send to Blogs By: _______________________________

Send to Betas By: _______________________________

Send to Editor By: _______________________________

Send to Formatter By: _______________________________

Set Up Pre-Order/Release By: _______________________________

Final Cover Design Needed By: _______________________________

Upload By: _______________________________

Extra Notes:

____

____

____

____

Book Title: _______________________________

Release Date: _______________________________

Cover Reveal: _______________________________

ARC Release: _______________________________

Send to Pre-Reader(s) By: _______________________________

Send to Blogs By: _______________________________

Send to Betas By: _______________________________

Send to Editor By: _______________________________

Send to Formatter By: _______________________________

Set Up Pre-Order/Release By: _______________________________

Final Cover Design Needed By: _______________________________

Upload By: _______________________________

Extra Notes:

____

____

____

____

____

Book Title: _______________________________

Release Date: _______________________________

Cover Reveal: _______________________________

ARC Release: _______________________________

Send to Pre-Reader(s) By: _______________________________

Send to Blogs By: _______________________________

Send to Betas By: _______________________________

Send to Editor By: _______________________________

Send to Formatter By: _______________________________

Set Up Pre-Order/Release By: _______________________________

Final Cover Design Needed By: _______________________________

Upload By: _______________________________

Extra Notes:

____

____

____

____

____

Book Title: _______________________________

Release Date: _______________________________

Cover Reveal: _______________________________

ARC Release: _______________________________

Send to Pre-Reader(s) By: _______________________________

Send to Blogs By: _______________________________

Send to Betas By: _______________________________

Send to Editor By: _______________________________

Send to Formatter By: _______________________________

Set Up Pre-Order/Release By: _______________________________

Final Cover Design Needed By: _______________________________

Upload By: _______________________________

Extra Notes:

____

____

____

____

Book Title: ___________________________

Release Date: ___________________________

Cover Reveal: ___________________________

ARC Release: ___________________________

Send to Pre-Reader(s) By: ___________________________

Send to Blogs By: ___________________________

Send to Betas By: ___________________________

Send to Editor By: ___________________________

Send to Formatter By: ___________________________

Set Up Pre-Order/Release By: ___________________________

Final Cover Design Needed By: ___________________________

Upload By: ___________________________

Extra Notes:

____

____

____

____

____

Book Title: _______________________________

Release Date: _______________________________

Cover Reveal: _______________________________

ARC Release: _______________________________

Send to Pre-Reader(s) By: _______________________________

Send to Blogs By: _______________________________

Send to Betas By: _______________________________

Send to Editor By: _______________________________

Send to Formatter By: _______________________________

Set Up Pre-Order/Release By: _______________________________

Final Cover Design Needed By: _______________________________

Upload By: _______________________________

Extra Notes:

____

____

____

____

____

Book Title: ______________________________

Release Date: ______________________________

Cover Reveal: ______________________________

ARC Release: ______________________________

Send to Pre-Reader(s) By: ______________________________

Send to Blogs By: ______________________________

Send to Betas By: ______________________________

Send to Editor By: ______________________________

Send to Formatter By: ______________________________

Set Up Pre-Order/Release By: ______________________________

Final Cover Design Needed By: ______________________________

Upload By: ______________________________

Extra Notes:

____

____

____

____

____

Book Title: _______________________________

Release Date: _______________________________

Cover Reveal: _______________________________

ARC Release: _______________________________

Send to Pre-Reader(s) By: _______________________________

Send to Blogs By: _______________________________

Send to Betas By: _______________________________

Send to Editor By: _______________________________

Send to Formatter By: _______________________________

Set Up Pre-Order/Release By: _______________________________

Final Cover Design Needed By: _______________________________

Upload By: _______________________________

Extra Notes:

____

____

____

____

____

Book Title: _______________________________

Release Date: _______________________________

Cover Reveal: _______________________________

ARC Release: _______________________________

Send to Pre-Reader(s) By: _______________________________

Send to Blogs By: _______________________________

Send to Betas By: _______________________________

Send to Editor By: _______________________________

Send to Formatter By: _______________________________

Set Up Pre-Order/Release By: _______________________________

Final Cover Design Needed By: _______________________________

Upload By: _______________________________

Extra Notes:

____

____

____

____

____

Book Title: ___________________________

Release Date: ___________________________

Cover Reveal: ___________________________

ARC Release: ___________________________

Send to Pre-Reader(s) By: ___________________________

Send to Blogs By: ___________________________

Send to Betas By: ___________________________

Send to Editor By: ___________________________

Send to Formatter By: ___________________________

Set Up Pre-Order/Release By: ___________________________

Final Cover Design Needed By: ___________________________

Upload By: ___________________________

Extra Notes:

____

____

____

____

____

Book Title: _______________________________

Release Date: _______________________________

Cover Reveal: _______________________________

ARC Release: _______________________________

Send to Pre-Reader(s) By: _______________________________

Send to Blogs By: _______________________________

Send to Betas By: _______________________________

Send to Editor By: _______________________________

Send to Formatter By: _______________________________

Set Up Pre-Order/Release By: _______________________________

Final Cover Design Needed By: _______________________________

Upload By: _______________________________

Extra Notes:

____

____

____

____

____

Book Title: ______________________________

Release Date: ______________________________

Cover Reveal: ______________________________

ARC Release: ______________________________

Send to Pre-Reader(s) By: ______________________________

Send to Blogs By: ______________________________

Send to Betas By: ______________________________

Send to Editor By: ______________________________

Send to Formatter By: ______________________________

Set Up Pre-Order/Release By: ______________________________

Final Cover Design Needed By: ______________________________

Upload By: ______________________________

Extra Notes:

____

____

____

____

____

Book Title: ______________________________

Release Date: ______________________________

Cover Reveal: ______________________________

ARC Release: ______________________________

Send to Pre-Reader(s) By: ______________________________

Send to Blogs By: ______________________________

Send to Betas By: ______________________________

Send to Editor By: ______________________________

Send to Formatter By: ______________________________

Set Up Pre-Order/Release By: ______________________________

Final Cover Design Needed By: ______________________________

Upload By: ______________________________

Extra Notes:

____

____

____

____

BOOK TITLE: _______________________________________

RELEASE DATE: _______________________________________

COVER REVEAL: _______________________________________

ARC RELEASE: _______________________________________

SEND TO PRE-READER(S) BY: _______________________________________

SEND TO BLOGS BY: _______________________________________

SEND TO BETAS BY: _______________________________________

SEND TO EDITOR BY: _______________________________________

SEND TO FORMATTER BY: _______________________________________

SET UP PRE-ORDER/RELEASE BY: _______________________________________

FINAL COVER DESIGN NEEDED BY: _______________________________________

UPLOAD BY: _______________________________________

EXTRA NOTES:

____

____

____

____

Book Title: ___________________________________

Release Date: ___________________________________

Cover Reveal: ___________________________________

ARC Release: ___________________________________

Send to Pre-Reader(s) By: ___________________________________

Send to Blogs By: ___________________________________

Send to Betas By: ___________________________________

Send to Editor By: ___________________________________

Send to Formatter By: ___________________________________

Set Up Pre-Order/Release By: ___________________________________

Final Cover Design Needed By: ___________________________________

Upload By: ___________________________________

Extra Notes:

____

____

____

____

Book Title: _______________________________

Release Date: _______________________________

Cover Reveal: _______________________________

ARC Release: _______________________________

Send to Pre-Reader(s) By: _______________________________

Send to Blogs By: _______________________________

Send to Betas By: _______________________________

Send to Editor By: _______________________________

Send to Formatter By: _______________________________

Set Up Pre-Order/Release By: _______________________________

Final Cover Design Needed By: _______________________________

Upload By: _______________________________

Extra Notes:

____

____

____

____

____

Book Title: _______________________________

Release Date: _______________________________

Cover Reveal: _______________________________

ARC Release: _______________________________

Send to Pre-Reader(s) By: _______________________________

Send to Blogs By: _______________________________

Send to Betas By: _______________________________

Send to Editor By: _______________________________

Send to Formatter By: _______________________________

Set Up Pre-Order/Release By: _______________________________

Final Cover Design Needed By: _______________________________

Upload By: _______________________________

Extra Notes:

____

____

____

____

____

Book Title: ______________________________

Release Date: ______________________________

Cover Reveal: ______________________________

ARC Release: ______________________________

Send to Pre-Reader(s) By: ______________________________

Send to Blogs By: ______________________________

Send to Betas By: ______________________________

Send to Editor By: ______________________________

Send to Formatter By: ______________________________

Set Up Pre-Order/Release By: ______________________________

Final Cover Design Needed By: ______________________________

Upload By: ______________________________

Extra Notes:

____

____

____

____

____

Book Title: ______________________________

Release Date: ______________________________

Cover Reveal: ______________________________

ARC Release: ______________________________

Send to Pre-Reader(s) By: ______________________________

Send to Blogs By: ______________________________

Send to Betas By: ______________________________

Send to Editor By: ______________________________

Send to Formatter By: ______________________________

Set Up Pre-Order/Release By: ______________________________

Final Cover Design Needed By: ______________________________

Upload By: ______________________________

Extra Notes:

____

____

____

____

____

Book Title: ___________________________

Release Date: ___________________________

Cover Reveal: ___________________________

ARC Release: ___________________________

Send to Pre-Reader(s) By: ___________________________

Send to Blogs By: ___________________________

Send to Betas By: ___________________________

Send to Editor By: ___________________________

Send to Formatter By: ___________________________

Set Up Pre-Order/Release By: ___________________________

Final Cover Design Needed By: ___________________________

Upload By: ___________________________

Extra Notes:

____

____

____

____

____

Book Title: ______________________________

Release Date: ______________________________

Cover Reveal: ______________________________

ARC Release: ______________________________

Send to Pre-Reader(s) By: ______________________________

Send to Blogs By: ______________________________

Send to Betas By: ______________________________

Send to Editor By: ______________________________

Send to Formatter By: ______________________________

Set Up Pre-Order/Release By: ______________________________

Final Cover Design Needed By: ______________________________

Upload By: ______________________________

Extra Notes:

____

____

____

____

Book Title: _______________________________

Release Date: _______________________________

Cover Reveal: _______________________________

ARC Release: _______________________________

Send to Pre-Reader(s) By: _______________________________

Send to Blogs By: _______________________________

Send to Betas By: _______________________________

Send to Editor By: _______________________________

Send to Formatter By: _______________________________

Set Up Pre-Order/Release By: _______________________________

Final Cover Design Needed By: _______________________________

Upload By: _______________________________

Extra Notes:

____

____

____

____

____

BOOK TITLE: ________________________________

RELEASE DATE: ________________________________

COVER REVEAL: ________________________________

ARC RELEASE: ________________________________

SEND TO PRE-READER(S) BY: ________________________________

SEND TO BLOGS BY: ________________________________

SEND TO BETAS BY: ________________________________

SEND TO EDITOR BY: ________________________________

SEND TO FORMATTER BY: ________________________________

SET UP PRE-ORDER/RELEASE BY: ________________________________

FINAL COVER DESIGN NEEDED BY: ________________________________

UPLOAD BY: ________________________________

EXTRA NOTES:

____

____

____

____

Book Title: _______________________________

Release Date: _______________________________

Cover Reveal: _______________________________

ARC Release: _______________________________

Send to Pre-Reader(s) By: _______________________________

Send to Blogs By: _______________________________

Send to Betas By: _______________________________

Send to Editor By: _______________________________

Send to Formatter By: _______________________________

Set Up Pre-Order/Release By: _______________________________

Final Cover Design Needed By: _______________________________

Upload By: _______________________________

Extra Notes:

____

____

____

____

____

Book Title: ___________________________

Release Date: ___________________________

Cover Reveal: ___________________________

ARC Release: ___________________________

Send to Pre-Reader(s) By: ___________________________

Send to Blogs By: ___________________________

Send to Betas By: ___________________________

Send to Editor By: ___________________________

Send to Formatter By: ___________________________

Set Up Pre-Order/Release By: ___________________________

Final Cover Design Needed By: ___________________________

Upload By: ___________________________

Extra Notes:

____

____

____

____

____

BOOK TITLE: _______________________________

RELEASE DATE: _______________________________

COVER REVEAL: _______________________________

ARC RELEASE: _______________________________

SEND TO PRE-READER(S) BY: _______________________________

SEND TO BLOGS BY: _______________________________

SEND TO BETAS BY: _______________________________

SEND TO EDITOR BY: _______________________________

SEND TO FORMATTER BY: _______________________________

SET UP PRE-ORDER/RELEASE BY: _______________________________

FINAL COVER DESIGN NEEDED BY: _______________________________

UPLOAD BY: _______________________________

EXTRA NOTES:

____

____

____

____

____

Book Title: _______________________________________

Release Date: _______________________________________

Cover Reveal: _______________________________________

ARC Release: _______________________________________

Send to Pre-Reader(s) By: _______________________________________

Send to Blogs By: _______________________________________

Send to Betas By: _______________________________________

Send to Editor By: _______________________________________

Send to Formatter By: _______________________________________

Set Up Pre-Order/Release By: _______________________________________

Final Cover Design Needed By: _______________________________________

Upload By: _______________________________________

Extra Notes:

____

____

____

____

____

Thank you so much for your purchase.

I really do hope that this book has helped you,
even in some small way.

Would you like to see different designs/styles?

I am always very happy to hear from customers,
so please feel free to email me on

teeceedesignstudio@yahoo.com